Butterflies
for
Kiri

by Cathryn Falwell

Happy Birthday, Kiri!

With special thanks to Casey, Adrienne, and Becky,
and to Sheri and Marianne, owners of *The Bookworm*
in Gorham, Maine—C.F.

This edition is published by special arrangement with Lee & Low Books Inc., New York, NY.

Grateful acknowledgment is made to Lee & Low Books Inc., New York, NY, for permission to reprint *Butterflies for Kiri* by Cathryn Falwell. Copyright © 2003 by Cathryn Falwell.

Printed in the United States of America

ISBN 10 0-15-365116-4
ISBN 13 978-0-15-365116-8

1 2 3 4 5 6 7 8 9 10   025 17 16 14 13 12 11 10 09 08 07

For my Aunt Sandy, who sent me a box of beautiful papers for my birthday long ago. Love, C.

Kiri loved to draw and paint and make things.

On Kiri's birthday, Auntie Lu sent a special gift. It had a purple paper butterfly perched on the top. Inside was a package of colored paper squares and a book called *Origami: The Art of Paper Folding.* The book showed how to fold the papers into wonderful things. There was a turtle, a boat, a bird, and a butterfly just like the one Auntie Lu had made for Kiri's package.

ORIGAMI:
The Art of
Paper Fo___

Kiri gently slid the beautiful papers from the package. She spread them out like a rainbow—purples, pinks, blues, greens, yellows, oranges, and reds. Kiri ran her finger softly over the papers. They were as thin as butterfly wings.

Kiri opened the origami book and looked at the drawings inside. The book had diagrams that showed how to do each step.

There were FOLD arrows,

and UNFOLD arrows.

There were VALLEY FOLD lines that folded forward,

and MOUNTAIN FOLD lines that folded backward.

"Fold crisply!" the book said. "Crease sharply!"

Kiri looked at Auntie Lu's butterfly. It had crisp folds, just like the ones in the book. Kiri studied the diagrams. There were fifteen steps to make a butterfly.

Kiri chose a sheet of bright purple paper that matched Auntie Lu's butterfly. Then she looked at the first diagram and carefully folded her paper the same way—corner to corner—with a crisp, neat crease. Kiri looked at the next step and folded her paper in half again.

For the next step all the corners had to meet in the center. Kiri folded her paper, but the corners didn't match up. She tried again, but it was hard to get the folds just right and the old creases still showed. Kiri tried the next step, but the thin purple paper tore a little along an old crease line.

Her beautiful paper! A tear ran down her cheek. Wiping her eyes, Kiri tried the next fold. The paper tore again.

"It's ruined!" Kiri cried. She wanted to start over, but she was afraid of tearing another sheet. Sadly she gathered up the rest of the papers and slid them safely back into the package.

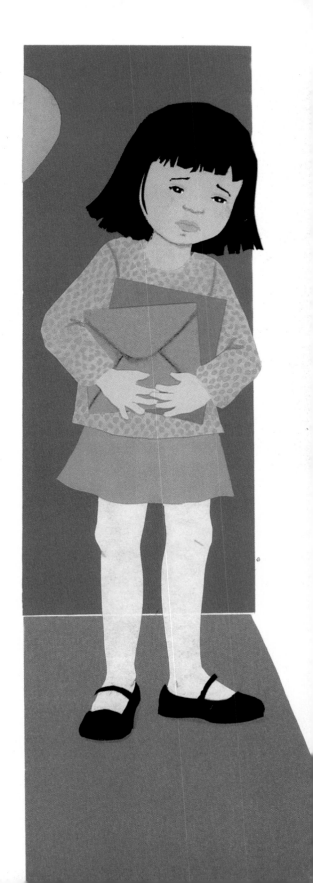

The next day Kiri carefully slid the origami papers from the package and spread them out like a rainbow—purples, pinks, blues, greens, yellows, oranges, and reds. The colors danced before her eyes.

Kiri wanted to try folding a butterfly again, but she didn't want to ruin another sheet of the beautiful papers. She took a piece of notebook paper and cut it into a square. Then very carefully Kiri followed the steps in the origami book. This time she got to the ninth step before the paper tore.

Some days after school
Kiri made chalk drawings.

Other days she painted,

or made things with clay.

And every day she practiced
making origami butterflies.

One Saturday morning Kiri went to the park to play.
It was a perfect spring day. She went high on a swing
and saw the bright blue sky and new green grass.
Pink petals from the trees blew gently in the breeze.

Kiri skipped by the bright red and purple tulips
shining up from the garden on her way home.
A yellow butterfly fluttered around the flowers.
The colors danced before Kiri's eyes. She couldn't
wait to get home to make a picture.

Quickly Kiri got out her watercolor paints, a brush, a jar of water, and a big sheet of paper. She dipped the brush into the water and then into the blue paint. With long strokes she painted the bright sky. She rinsed her brush and dipped it into the green paint. Slowly and carefully Kiri painted the spring grass.

Kiri rinsed her brush again, and this time she chose the red of the tulips. But as soon as her brush touched the grass, the red paint leaked into the wet green and made a muddy puddle. Kiri tried to scrub away the spot, but the paper got soggy and began to shred.

"It's terrible!" Kiri cried.

Mama came into the kitchen.

"I see the spring colors from the park," Mama said. "What a nice picture."

"No. It's ruined!" Kiri sobbed.

Kiri ran to her room. She was about to fling herself
onto her bed when she saw the package of origami papers.
Carefully she spread out the colors like a rainbow—purples,
pinks, blues, greens, yellows, oranges, and reds. There was
the bright red of the tulip she had tried to paint.

Kiri took her scissors and cut a shape from the corner
of the red paper. Then she took everything to the kitchen.

The red paper tulip looked perfect on her painting. Kiri smiled and glued the shape over the muddy spot. Scraps of purple, pink, blue, green, orange, and red floated onto the table as Kiri cut more and more shapes to add to her picture. The colors began to dance.

Kiri looked over her colored papers
again and chose a bright yellow square.
She took a deep breath and folded it . . .

. . . into a beautiful butterfly.

How to Make an  Origami Butterfly

1.
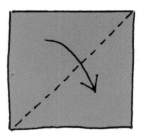
Fold a paper
square in half.

2.
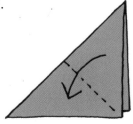
Fold it in half again.

3.

Unfold the paper.

4.
Fold all the corners
to the center.

5.
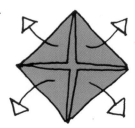
Unfold the
paper again.

6.
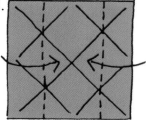
Fold the sides
into the center.

7.
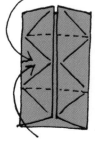
Fold the top and
bottom to the center.

8.

It should look
like this.

9.
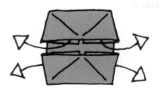
Carefully pull out the
inside corners.

10.
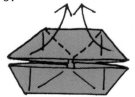
Press flat. Then fold
up the top corners.

11.
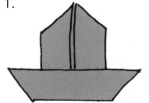
It should look
like this now.

12.
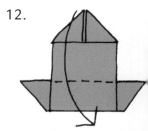
Turn it over and fold
down the top.

13.
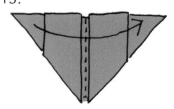
Now fold the whole
thing in half.

14.
Open by making a small
diagonal fold. Repeat on
the other side.

15.
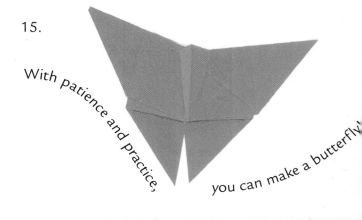
With patience and practice, you can make a butterfly!